50
of the Most Inspiring
African-Americans

50
of the Most Inspiring
African–Americans

Edited by Patricia M. Hinds ▪ Introduction by Susan L. Taylor

ESSENCE
BOOKS

Time Inc. Home Entertainment

Publisher: Richard Fraiman
Executive Director, Marketing Services: Carol Pittard
Director, Retail & Special Sales: Tom Mifsud
Marketing Director, Branded Businesses: Swati Rao
Director, New Product Development: Peter Harper
Financial Director: Steven Sandonato
Prepress Manager: Emily Rabin
Book Production Manager: Suzanne Janso
Associate Prepress Manager: Anne-Michelle Gallero
Assistant Marketing Managers: Alexandra Bliss, Calandria Wells

Special thanks: Bozena Bannett, Glenn Buonocore, Robert Marasco, Brooke McGuire, Jonathan Polsky, Chavaughn Raines, Ilene Schreider, Adriana Tierno, Britney Williams

Special thanks to Imaging: Patrick Dugan, Eddie Matros

We welcome your comments and suggestions about Essence Books. Please write to us at:
Essence Books
Attention: Book Editors
PO Box 11016
Des Moines, IA 50336-1016

If you would like to order any of our hardcover Collector's Edition books, please call us at 1-800-327-6388. (Monday through Friday, 7:00 a.m.- 8:00 p.m. or Saturday, 7:00 a.m.-6:00 p.m. Central Time).

CONTRIBUTORS

Editor-in-Chief: Patricia Hinds
Writers: Joy Duckett Cain, Deborah Gregory, Pamela Johnson,
Rosemarie Robotham, Diane Weathers
Assistant Editors: Myra McGriff, Nicole Sealey
Designers: Eve Sandler and Elyse Strongin/Sagebrush Studios, Janice Wheeler
Photo Researchers: Stephanie Dash, Myra McGriff
Copy Editors: Nana Badu, Sherrill Clarke, Hope Wright
Fact Checker: Shena Verrett
Administrative Assistants: Jeannette Reyes, Rozalynn S. Frazier

Produced and packaged by Mignon Communications

Special thanks: Susan L. Taylor, Michelle Ebanks, Ed Lewis, LaToya Valmont,
Angela Burt-Murray, Vanessa Bush, Fred Allen, Jan deChabert, Karen Brown,
Marsha Kelly, LaVon Leak-Wilks, Kathryn Leary, Sandra Martin, Debra
Parker, Charlotte Wiggers

Acknowledgments: Greg Alford, Gregory Boyea, Edgerton Maloney,
Larry Ramo, Leah Rudolfo

TABLE OF CONTENTS

Our Power, Our Purpose

THE women and men you will find in this book are a special breed, wise souls who appreciate the profound gift of being alive. They come from every sector of society; they represent the worlds of entertainment, education, business, religion, politics and activism. Some are known and lauded throughout the world; others are working quietly in their communities, expecting no praise, wanting only to serve. All are using the strength and the talent God gave them, working in their own ways to fulfill their destiny and make a difference in the lives of others and in the life of our world.

These 50 inspiring African-Americans have achieved public or private greatness by living to the fullest, understanding that God has given each of us the creative intelligence to make everything better, within ourselves and everywhere around us. They accept the deep truth that anything broken can be mended, can be made whole again, can be made even better than before. They know that God wants us to practice love and compassion. They know too that adversity has its place and that when things fall apart, as they inevitably will at times, it is never to punish us. It is always for our instruction, to help us grow in wisdom, faith and courage; to strengthen our spirit and resolve so that we may become ever more perfect vessels, using our lives for the greatest good.

It is this message of perseverance and striving and love that inspired this book. We wanted to put this volume in the hands of our people—of all people—as a testament to our individual power and reminder of our higher purpose. No people on earth have suffered as gravely or for as long as we have. But we have survived, and here we are, the privileged ones for whom the generations before us sacrificed, struggled and kept the faith. A book about Black achievement is critical now, because everything that our foreparents wanted for their children can now be ours. We have arrived at that moment in our history they so hoped for. Everything we need to live fully, everything necessary to our individual well-being and the well-being of our families and our communities, lies waiting for us to claim. But we must believe in ourselves and in the boundless ability God has given us to revive and renew ourselves emotionally, physically and spiritually along the way.

Each person profiled in this book is, like us, living a life filled with unending challenge and change. Like the sisters and brothers in these pages, we have to clear away the subconscious patterns and beliefs that undermine our best intentions and weaken our trust in the essential goodness of life. We must learn to embrace our own power and intuition; we must never fear change. Instead, we must stay committed to learning, to finding the lessons in change, even as we devise new strategies for moving our lives forward. When we approach our lives in this way, we increase our energy, heighten our creativity and deepen our capacity for joy. We find, at last, the wisdom and the will to do the work God created us to do—to link arms and join in the purpose of ending the pain and suffering of so many around us. We find love.

It is my hope, and the hope of my ESSENCE family, that the stories and voices in this book will inspire us all to keep growing and moving forward in our lives. It is my hope that, through the example of these extraordinary women and men, we may find our own power and purpose—and also the conviction that together we can achieve the happiness and prosperity God has promised us, in a world of everlasting peace.

SUSAN L. TAYLOR

1

ICONS

They have broken records, won awards and, in the process, gained international fame and affection.

Denzel Washington

Halle Berry

AS Halle Berry wept during her Oscar acceptance speech for Best Actress of 2002 for her role in *Monster's Ball,* it seemed unfathomable that it took Hollywood 74 years to find a sister worthy of the Academy Award category, but it did. So Berry savored that moment of validation for *all* Black actresses. After years of having her place

> *"What's hardest for me to swallow is when they say, 'We love Halle— we just don't want to go Black with this part.'"*

in Hollywood questioned, Berry has reached a career high—all because she refused to accept the word *no.*

It's her resilience that we admire most. "What's hardest for me to swallow is when they say, 'We love Halle—we just don't want to go Black with this part.'" So when Hollywood offered limited roles, she created her own. She invested seven years in bringing the story about the 1950s movie star Dorothy Dandridge to film. She struggled to retain the story rights and negotiated with Home Box Office (HBO) to produce it. In 1999 Berry not only executive-produced the television movie *Introducing Dorothy Dandridge,* but she also played the lead role. She was later rewarded with a Golden Globe and an Emmy for her portrayal of the beloved actress.

Berry has repeatedly knocked down doors, insisting that directors re-envision her—and they have. Whether playing a grimy-faced crack addict in *Jungle Fever,* a sci-fi heroine in *X-Men* or a sexy spy in the James Bond film, *Die Another Day,* Berry has proven that she is much more than a pretty face. She has the talent and persistence that won't be stopped. ▪

Oprah Winfrey

OPRAH Winfrey is a one-woman revolution. Born on a farm with no indoor plumbing in Kosciusko, Mississippi, she cut through the ugly ways of segregation with a power that has lighted her path and ours. Her blend of wisdom and insight is dispensed daily on *The Oprah Winfrey Show*, seen on TV in more than 30 million homes in 115 countries. Winfrey has become a beacon for people with real life struggles, those who have had a love and lost it, gone on a diet but couldn't stick to it, tried something new and been criticized for it. Indeed she has changed our lives. She taught sisters to dream, sisters who had never seen anyone like her on TV—powerful, independent and still a down-home girl.

Winfrey has become a beacon for those who have had a love and lost it, gone on a diet but couldn't stick to it, tried something new and been criticized for it.

Her countless fans have followed as Winfrey has made inroads into publishing, film and philanthropy. Oprah's Angel Network, a campaign that encourages viewers to donate to the needy, has collected millions of dollars for college scholarships, individual grants and for building homes in support of Habitat for Humanity. Her generosity also has brought hope and love to African children.

Her book club has championed reading throughout the U.S and abroad, proving to be a godsend for authors and the publishing industry. On the strength of Winfrey's recommendation, books become instant bestsellers. And the launch of *O, The Oprah Magazine* was the most successful magazine launch in this country. Winfrey has also excelled in acting and producing movies and was nominated for an Academy Award for her performance as Sofia in *The Color Purple*. She executive-produced several big- and small-screen movies

Oprah Winfrey has amassed millions of loyal fans who tune in to her show.

including *Beloved* and *Their Eyes Were Watching God*. In another role, she is a founder of Oxygen Media, which includes a women's cable network.

Ahead of her time, at age 3, Winfrey was reciting Scripture in church. At 17, as Miss Fire Prevention in Nashville, she stopped by the local radio station, read the news for a lark and so impressed the managers that they hired her. Two years later, in her sophomore year at Tennessee State University, Winfrey became the first woman and first African-American television-news anchor in Nashville's history. That was just the beginning of her groundbreaking achievements.

In 1984, after a short stint in Baltimore, the Windy City summoned, welcoming Winfrey as the host of *AM Chicago*. The program quickly became the number one TV talk show in the city, and less than a year later, it was renamed *The Oprah Winfrey Show*. Since 1986 it has been the top-rated talk show in the country. She's the first Black woman ever to own a television studio and our first Black woman billionaire. Thanks to Oprah, the revolution is being televised. ▪

Michael Jordan

WHEN Michael Jordan was in high school, he was cut from his varsity basketball team. But that didn't stop him from becoming one of the greatest basketball players of all time. Jordan has passed from sports icon to pure phenomenon.

> "I can accept failure, but I can't accept not trying."

As a college freshman, he made the game-winning shot that earned his University of North Carolina team the NCAA championship. After his junior year, Jordan was drafted by the Chicago Bulls, where he won ten scoring titles and helped his team win six NBA championships. His skill made him the darling of Madison Avenue; his savoir faire made him the people's choice.

But in 1993, at the height of Jordan's athletic success, his beloved father was killed, prompting Jordan to reassess his life. In 1994, after leaving the game, Jordan, in honor and memory of his father, gave $2 million to build Chicago's 41,000-square-foot James R. Jordan Boys and Girls Club and Family Center. Two years later he donated $1 million to his alma mater to launch the Jordan Institute for Families, part of the university's School of Social Work.

His philanthropic deeds are tremendous, as is his love of the game. In 1995 he returned to the Chicago Bulls and led the team in some of the most spectacular seasons in NBA history. He retired again in 1999. Later Jordan became part owner of the Washington Wizards team, but couldn't stay on the sidelines for long and came back as a player before retiring in 2003. As in his high school years, Jordan lives by his mantra, "I can accept failure, but I can't accept not trying." ▪

With unique grace, power and style, Michael Jordan has redefined the role of the athlete in popular culture.

Jordan's mother, Deloris, joins Michael in supporting a variety of family-related charities.

Janet Jackson

WE know every move of the public Janet Jackson, but there is no spotlight on her when she performs charitable work. And more than anyone fully knows, she shares her abundant blessings with those who face poverty, disease and war. Jackson gives generously to service organizations, has donated proceeds of concerts to African relief funds and visits suffering children. And she is a supporter of America's Promise—The Alliance for Youth, a nonprofit organization that works to help children live and learn in a safe environment. Jackson, a child star who grew up to be a megastar, is dedicated to making a difference in the lives of children in need.

Jackson first strutted onstage as the baby sister and sidekick of her famous brothers, the Jackson Five. Now, more than two decades later, she stands solidly alone. One of the most popular performers in the world, she has made her mark in television and film and as a megahit singer and talented dancer. Her album sales top more than 50 million worldwide. Janet's trendsetting videos have set the standard in the industry.

More than anyone fully knows, Jackson shares her abundant blessings with those who face poverty, disease and war.

As a preteen, she enjoyed success in roles on the television sitcoms *Good Times* and *Different Strokes*, and later in the drama *Fame*. But Jackson wanted more. She wanted to be a star and to be known for her own work and talent. When her 1982 debut album didn't create the stir she had hoped for, it didn't stop her. She worked harder.

In 1986, under the guidance of her now-longtime producing partners Terry Lewis and Jimmy Jam, Jackson wowed the music industry with the release of *Control*. She presented fans with tracks like "What Have You Done

From apple-cheeked child star to world-class entertainer, Janet has conquered music, television and film.

for Me Lately" that left no question about what the baby of the Jackson family demanded—respect. *Control* made it to No. 1 on the pop and R&B charts.

Holding the reins to her musical future, Janet continued to top the charts. In 1989 *Rhythm Nation 1814* produced four No. 1 singles, including "Miss You Much" and three Top 5 hits. In 1993 the album *Janet* earned six Top 10 hits, and her 1997 *Velvet Rope*, the chart-topping *All For You* in 2001, as well as the more recent *Damita Jo* have helped to secure her place in music history. She has more than proven her talent and versatility—she has proven that she alone determines her destiny.

Not only does Janet Jackson give her all to her fans, but as a philanthropist she has also spread her gifts to make a difference in the lives of many more. ∎

Muhammad Ali

WHEN Muhammad Ali was still a kid, he spoke with the confidence of the three-time heavyweight boxing champ he would one day become. He bragged about himself long before he earned bragging rights. And he hit the airwaves with a barrage of poetic self-promotion that made folks laugh and stay riveted to his every move.

But Ali, known as Cassius Clay before his 1964 conversion to Islam, was not in the fight game solely for the flash or the cash. He always stood for something greater. At 18 years of age, he won the gold medal in boxing for America during the Summer Olympics in Rome. But he parted with the coveted medal on principle, tossing it into a river after he was refused service at a lunch counter in Louisville because he was Black. Some people shunned him when he joined the Nation of Islam. And when the U.S. Army threatened to imprison him if he did not go to war in Vietnam, he refused to bend. "I ain't got no quarrel with the Viet Cong," he said. "No Viet Cong never called me a nigger." Ali was sentenced to five years in prison and stripped of his heavyweight title. His future seemed uncertain. Fortunately he was released on appeal and his conviction was overturned three years later. But those prime years as an athlete were lost.

Ali came out slugging, giving the world some of the most exciting and entertaining boxing matches it has ever seen. His 1971 winning fight against Joe Frazier was billed as the "Fight of the Century," and in his 1974 "Rumble in the Jungle" with George Foreman in Zaire, he became only the second heavyweight champion in history to regain his title.

Now Ali faces his toughest battle yet with Parkinson's disease. He is called The Greatest not only for his astonishing athletic ability, but also for his courage to risk fame and fortune to stand by his convictions and his people. ■

Three-time heavyweight champion Muhammad Ali is one of the world's most recognizable icons.

Denzel Washington

EVEN with $20 million film deals and two Oscars, Denzel Washington doesn't forget that he was once a kid hanging out at the Boys and Girls Club of Mount Vernon, New York, struggling to find a sense of direction. As one of the most successful actors in Hollywood, he opens his heart and gives time and money to the Boys and Girls Clubs of America to help kids who are just like he was. He and his wife, Pauletta, are also passionate supporters of their church community, African children's charities and organizations that help to ease life's burdens on those less fortunate.

Odds were certainly not in his favor when he showed up in Hollywood more than two decades ago. But his astonishing talent and perseverance have boosted him to the top, proving without a doubt that he is an exceptional actor. From his masterful performance in *Malcolm X* to the homophobic lawyer for a dying gay client in *Philadelphia* to the runaway slave in *Glory* (for which he won an Academy Award for Best Supporting Actor), he is the consummate artist. His portrayal of a bad-to-the-bone police officer in *Training Day* brought him an Academy Award for Best Actor—at that time only the second in that esteemed category won by an African-American male in the Academy's 74-year history.

Back in the day, as a student at New York City's Fordham University, Washington had planned a journalism career. But after performing in student productions, he was bitten by the acting bug. At the Actors' Conservatory Theater in San Francisco, he quickly excelled, and after only one year, Washington stepped out on faith, moving 500 miles down the road to Hollywood.

> *"The things we have are not of my own doing. I am not the reason we have these things; God is."*

Denzel Washington, married to Pauletta, was a stage actor before becoming a film star.

The father of four children, Washington says raising grounded kids in Hollywood requires that he be present and vigilant. "I try to explain to them that all they see around us, the things we have, are not of my own doing," he says. "I am not the reason we have these things; God is. I want them to realize that you don't have to stab anybody in the back. You don't have to scratch anybody's eyes out. Just be honest, work hard and have faith. That will take them farther in life. ∎

2

POWER BROKERS

They have defied convention to rise to extraordinary heights and to wield potent political influence.

Barack Obama

IN his late father's native Swahili, Barack means "one who is blessed by God." And there's no question that Barack Obama's blessings are abundant. In the eyes of many political observers, he might well be the leader of a new generation.

> *At the age of 43, he became the country's only African-American senator and only the third since Reconstruction.*

He was a little-known state senator representing Chicago's South Side and making an ambitious run for the U.S. Senate when he was tapped to deliver the keynote speech at the Democratic Convention in 2004. He moved many people in the audience to tears and thunderous applause when he called on the nation to put aside the divisive rhetoric and instead take a stand for unity. "There is not a liberal America and a conservative America," he said. "There is the United States of America. There is not a Black America and a White America and Latino America and Asian America; there's the United States of America."

In the November elections, he would claim a sweeping victory, defeating Republican candidate Alan Keyes by winning 70 percent of the vote. At the age of 43, he became the country's only African-American senator and only the third since Reconstruction.

Born in Hawaii to a Kenyan father and a White American mother from Kansas, Obama is well aware that he represents the face of a new, more diverse generation. "All of these different strains in me—the Black, the White, the African—all of that has contributed directly to my success, because when I meet people, I see a piece

Senator Barack
Obama is always
interested in knowing
the concerns of
the people in his
Chicago community.

of myself in them," he says. "And maybe they see a piece of themselves in me."

Obama wasn't always so self-assured. His father left the family when he was a baby, and the two would meet only once after that. *In Dreams From My Father,* his best-selling autobiography, he describes how his struggle with adolescence and his multiethnic background led him to experiment with drugs and alcohol. Eventually he would graduate from Columbia University and work as a community organizer in Chicago. He went on to Harvard Law School, where he became the first African-American editor of its prestigious law review.

Senator Obama, who serves on the Environment and Public Works and Veterans Affairs Committees, hasn't discussed his political aspirations publicly. But that hasn't kept others from doing it. The campaign mugs, posters, bumper stickers, buttons and T-shirts are already printed touting him for president. They say: *Barack Obama in 2008.* ■

Senator Obama and his wife, Michelle, share a light moment before he delivered the keynote address at the Democratic National Convention.

Congresswoman
Waters won't
rest until all
people of color
are politically
active.

Maxine Waters

SHE is a gutsy street fighter and a fierce advocate for Black and Latino empowerment. During her seven terms as a Democratic congresswoman from the thirty-fifth district in California (South Central Los Angeles, Watts), Representative Maxine Waters has fearlessly addressed a range of vital issues that affect people of color.

The fifth of 13 children, Waters was raised in St. Louis by a single mother. It was a struggle to make ends meet and the family went on welfare. After high school, Waters married and moved to Los Angeles, where she raised two children. She became more involved with her community while working as a Head Start teacher's assistant. In 1976 Waters was elected to the California State Assembly and, after serving for 14 years, ran for Congress in 1990 and won. When the 1992 riots broke out in her district following the Rodney King verdict, the nation watched as Waters, one of the first politicians on the scene, delivered relief supplies. And she has stood alone in demanding an investigation into the CIA's alleged involvement in flooding urban areas with drugs.

> *"There are many brave African-Americans. They need to be inspired by those of us who have a platform."*

Maxine Waters has battled urban poverty, fought to create new jobs and worked to restore abandoned buildings in her district. She has publicized the importance of computer literacy and spoken loud and long about the devastating effects of drugs in our cities. The congresswoman has teamed with other members of the Congressional Black Caucus to address the AIDS crisis in the Black community, resulting in the HIV/AIDS Initiative, a program to support prevention, education and treatment services nationwide.

And she has brought hip-hop artists and gang members to the table. But she won't rest until we're all politically active, she says. "I am blessed and I want to afford opportunities to my people," Waters states. "There are many brave African-Americans. They need to be inspired by those of us who have a platform." ▩

Kwame Kilpatrick

KWAME Kilpatrick was a state representative for Detroit's west side, an up-and-comer who had been chosen as the first African-American to lead the Michigan House Democratic Caucus. But in his soul, being a representative and serving in the House wasn't enough. Kilpatrick wanted to become mayor, even though he knew people would consider him too young.

One night, while trying to decide whether to run for office, Kilpatrick opened up the Bible to the page that described David's taking control of the land of Judah at age 30. For Kilpatrick, who is married and the father of three sons, it was clearly a sign from God. "That night I decided to run, and I felt better," he says. "No more butterflies, no more nervousness. It was time to move on with the mission." Kilpatrick campaigned vigorously. He promised to focus on improving schools, fighting crime and restoring neighborhoods. He shook hands and charmed his constituents, telling anecdotes about how he obeyed his elders and wanted to serve the people of Detroit. It was a close race, pitting a veteran councilman against a political wunderkind. But in November 2001, the 31-year-old won. After his victory, Kilpatrick, the youngest mayor in Detroit history, initiated new and improved housing, roads and infrastructure, and he sparked the revival of neighborhoods, including downtown.

Kilpatrick first set foot in the mayor's office as a 10-year-old, when he interviewed Mayor Coleman Young for a school essay. He had become interested in politics two years earlier when he helped his mother, activist Carolyn Cheeks Kilpatrick, successfully campaign for the state House. Kilpatrick attended Florida A&M on a football scholarship, graduated with honors, then taught in the Detroit public-school system before taking a job in private industry. When the lure of politics became too strong to ignore, he ran for his mother's former seat in the state legislature.

Kilpatrick's experience proves two things: First, age ain't nothing but a number, and second, we owe it to ourselves to live our vision and follow our hearts. ■

"No more butterflies, no more nervousness. It was time to move on with the mission."

Shirley Franklin

IT'S not easy for a sister to break into the old boys' network, much less lead it. But here is a woman who broke through with her own style and purpose.

That's what happened when Atlantans elected Shirley Franklin as mayor in November 2001. During the campaign, Franklin, who dyed her salt-and-pepper hair blond, sometimes used hip-hop beats as background music in her election ads. She had folks as diverse as Governor Roy Barnes of Georgia, writer Maya Angelou and the rap group

> *It's not easy for a sister to break the old boys' network, but she did— with style and purpose.*

Outkast in her corner. Certainly you had to give the diminutive sister (she's five feet tall) points for style. But Atlantans quickly realized that Franklin also deserved props for substance.

Franklin's career in public service began in Atlanta in 1978 as Mayor Maynard Jackson's commissioner of cultural affairs. She was later appointed the nation's first woman city manager during Mayor Andrew Young's tenure, a job in which she managed Atlanta's billion-dollar budget and nearly 8,000 employees. When Franklin ran for mayor, it was this job experience that she emphasized. She won fans across the board by addressing the tough issues such as the city's $92 million budget gap and its crumbling bridges and sewer system. Her strategy worked: She won more than 50 percent of the vote. Mayor Franklin's goals included improving Atlanta's mostly Black public schools and building coalitions among its Black, White and Asian populations. In running for office, Franklin successfully reached out to all segments of the population. "I knew I would appeal to the majority of people who are not eager to return to the time when people didn't get along," Franklin says of her broad-based support. "I don't think that's a move away from race, but a move toward inclusiveness." ■

With "blonde ambition," Shirley Franklin became Atlanta's first African-American female to hold the office of mayor.

As national
security advisor,
Condoleezza Rice
has the ear
of the president.

Condoleezza Rice

IT'S a great journey Condoleezza Rice has made, from the Jim Crow South to a corner office in the White House. She is one of the most powerful women in the world. The nation's first woman and the first African-American national security advisor, in 2005 she became the first Black woman secretary of state. Rice has great influence on the president of the United States. She is a top advisor

> *Condoleezza Rice is one of the most powerful women in the world.*

to President George W. Bush on foreign affairs and his guide and counsel on world politics. Rice also counseled the senior George Bush when he was president and helped create many of the U.S. policies in the wake of the reunification of Germany and the final days of the Soviet Union.

The power to focus has always put her at the head of her class. Rice skipped the first and seventh grades, and entered the University

of Denver at 15, graduating cum laude four years later with a degree in political science. A Soviet specialist who is fluent in Russian, she applied that same drive to earn master's and Ph.D. degrees. She became a professor at Stanford University in 1981 and served as provost in the 1990s.

Much rests on her shoulders, but she is humble about the source of her strength. "I'm a deeply religious person," she has said. "I was taught that you don't pray with a laundry list, so I ask for wisdom and guidance and strength of conviction." ■

Colin completed
two tours of
Vietnam, where
he earned two
Purple Hearts.

Colin Powell

COLIN Powell embodies the best of the American dream. The son of Jamaican immigrants who grew up on the rough streets of the Bronx became the nation's first Black secretary of state. Powell, who was appointed by President George W. Bush, served as his chief foreign-affairs advisor. Presidents Reagan, Bush (senior) and Clinton also sought his wise counsel. As a master strategist and a fair and respected negotiator, Powell has been involved in the United States' most critical international conflicts—Panama, Desert Storm, Kosovo, the Middle East and the war on terrorism. His accomplishments would be amazing for even the best and the brightest, but especially so for the self-described "Black kid of no early promise and limited means."

> *"In one generation we have moved from denying a Black man service at a lunch counter to elevating one to the highest military office in the nation."*

The road to greatness began with one small step: Powell enrolled in the Army's ROTC program at City College of New York, where he says he discovered his mission: to serve his country. After he completed two tours in Vietnam, where he was wounded twice and earned two Purple Hearts, his bravery helped him rise rapidly through the ranks: He became a general at the relatively young age of 42, and later a four-star general. A professional soldier for 35 years, Powell was appointed Chairman of the Joint Chiefs of Staff, the highest military position in the Department of Defense, from which he oversaw the Persian Gulf War.

In 1993 Colin Powell retired from the military, and the devoted husband and family man focused on writing his autobiography, *My American Journey*. The bestseller launched him as a popular speaker here and abroad. Buoyed by his popularity, he considered running for the nation's highest office and was courted by Democrats and Republicans alike. Never one to be seduced by power, however, he ultimately reaffirmed that the path he had been on was the right one.

Powell was the founding chairman of America's Promise, a national campaign to get adults invested in the lives of our children, to create safe places for kids to live and learn and to ensure that their free time includes skill building for the future.

Looking back at his journey, Powell, who retired in 2004, says, "In one generation we have moved from denying a Black man service at a lunch counter to elevating one to the highest military office in the nation and to being a serious contender for the presidency. This is a magnificent country, and I am proud to be one of its sons." ■

Colin Powell and his wife, Alma, support programs that invest in the lives of our children.

3

TRAILBLAZERS

Boldly forging into new territories,
they have staked unique claims,
taking care of business in the process.

Kenneth Gamble

Valerie Daniels-Carter leads the country's largest African-American–owned restaurant franchise.

Valerie Daniels-Carter

IN 1984 Valerie Daniels-Carter knew very little about the business of fast-food restaurants, but she knew an opportunity when she saw one—and she saw one in Burger King. Armed with a strong business background and a solid education, she was ready to nurture her entrepreneurial spirit. And the $95 million fast-food empire that has resulted is a mighty testament to one sister's willingness to step boldly into uncharted waters. Daniels-Carter leads the country's largest African-American–owned restaurant franchise.

While working as a commercial loan officer at a bank, Daniels-Carter teamed with her brother John to form V&J Holding Companies. They borrowed money and used savings (total cost: $750,000, including a $40,000 franchise fee) to build and equip their first Burger King restaurant in Milwaukee. They learned the ropes—sometimes on their own—along the way. "The industry was a challenge," she says. "I faced barriers that hadn't been broken through by a Black woman. And no one took me under his wing."

> *"It's extremely rewarding to have an organization that's recognized as being a large employer of people of color."*

But Daniels-Carter soared. In 1997 she bought 61 Pizza Hut restaurants, the largest transaction ever involving a Black woman and the chain. Today her 137 Burger King and Pizza Hut restaurants employ more than 3,000 people, many from inner-city communities of Michigan, Virginia, New York, Massachusetts and Wisconsin. "It's extremely rewarding to have an organization that's recognized as being a large employer of people of color," she says. ■

Cathy Hughes

WITH a string of firsts marking her career in the radio industry, Cathy Hughes has emerged as first lady of the airwaves, not just in the nation's capital, but also across the land. Consider her achievements: As founder and chairperson of the Washington, D.C., area–based Radio One, Inc., she heads the largest African-American–owned and operated broadcasting company in the country and the first African-American company in radio history to dominate several major markets. Hers is also the first woman-owned radio station to rank number one in any major market. And when she and her son, Alfred Liggins, president and CEO of Radio One, took the company public in 1999, she became the first African-American woman with a company on the stock exchange.

At 17 Hughes became a mother, but that didn't stop her from setting her goals. Three years later, with high school behind her and a few college courses under her belt, she helped a group of African-Americans acquire and run a radio station.

> *She used her microphone as a secular pulpit, championing the causes of our people and chiding America when the nation was too slow to act.*

Over the years Hughes began to take on a series of on-air and management positions. In her first year as general sales manager for WHUR, the Howard University–owned radio station, she increased the station's revenues from $250,000 to $3 million. There she also developed the sensuous late-night music format called The Quiet Storm, which is now an urban-radio staple.

Her belief in herself and her service to the Black community have led her to the big leagues. Hughes's 70 stations employ more than 2,200 people and reach more than 13 million listeners daily. In 2004 she launched TV One, a cable channel for African-Americans. She proves that Black women can not only run their own businesses, but can also turn them into mighty institutions. ■

"To rebuild a community, you have to rebuild the people, because the people are the community."

Kenneth Gamble

SHARING his soul was only the beginning for producer and songwriter Kenny Gamble. For more than a decade, the legendary innovator partnered with Leon Huff and gave us The Sound of Philadelphia, a distinctive brand of R&B that became America's sound track for the seventies and early eighties. The music, recorded by Harold Melvin and the Blue Notes, Phyllis Hyman, the O'Jays, Wilson Pickett, Teddy Pendergrass and so many more, had the whole world snapping its fingers. But the grooves went deeper, offering enduring messages about faith, love and life. Gamble and Huff's magic produced more than 3,000 songs and more than 170 gold- and platinum-selling records, many minted on their Black-owned Philadelphia International Records label.

Social change provided another important thematic element in their music. But Gamble was never content to leave it at that. Beginning in the seventies, he demonstrated an even higher commitment to Black people by buying run-down homes in his old south Philadelphia neighborhood and renovating them for disadvantaged families. In all, he has acquired more than 100 houses, including the one in which he grew up.

In 1990 Gamble moved out of his mansion and returned to his old south Philly community to oversee the turn-around. Through Universal Companies, his nonprofit organization, he provides job training, adult education and drug rehabilitation, as well as affordable homes for low- and moderate-income families. Gamble has also stepped forward as a local leader by heading up the Universal Institute Charter School.

"To rebuild a community," says Gamble, "in addition to the housing, you have to rebuild the people, because the people are the community." ▪

Kenneth Gamble's music offers soulful messages of faith, love and life.

Janice Bryant Howroyd

HOW do you turn a $1,500 investment into a $260 million business? Ask Janice Bryant Howroyd. Her vision of success took root in 1978, when she took her savings of $967 and a loan of $533 from family and used it to start Act 1 Personnel Services in Beverly Hills, California. The seed money paid for one month's rent and telephone service, and with brother Carlton's financial mentoring, the company grew and profits were reinvested. Today her company has 70 offices nationwide and is the largest Black-female–owned employment service in the country.

Howroyd, a Tarboro, North Carolina, native, knows it pays to diversify. Her business now includes a personnel agency, a graphic-design service, engineering management and a company that performs background checks. She employs more than 65,000 temporary workers and has more than three hundred full-time employees.

By sponsoring students at historically Black colleges and universities, including her own alma mater, North Carolina A&T State University, Howroyd is helping to create the next generation of businessmen and businesswomen. She has donated more than $20 million to universities. "African-Americans should have an entrepreneurial approach to their lives regardless of how they're employed and who signs their checks," she says. "I grasped the dream and created a reality for myself, and in so doing gave opportunity and value to others." ▪

> "I grasped the dream and created a reality for myself, and in so doing gave opportunity and value to others."

4

COMMUNITY BUILDERS

They are the activists, community leaders and visionaries—the ones in the trenches doing the critical work.

Yvonne Pointer

4 Mothers Against Violence

FRANCES DAVIS ▪ DEE SUMPTER ▪ YVONNE POINTER ▪ CHARLOTTE AUSTIN-JORDAN

FRANCES Davis, Dee Sumpter, Yvonne Pointer, Charlotte Austin-Jordan. They are charter members of a club no one wants to join, yet despite their wounded hearts, they are helping many others to heal theirs. After Frances Davis, Dee Sumpter, Yvonne Pointer and Charlotte Austin-Jordan lost children to violence, each woman turned her grief into a springboard to help others. "You can't run from the bloodshed," says Davis, who lost three sons in separate acts of gun violence. "You must stand where you are and fight." The catastrophe in Davis's life moved her to codirect Parents United to Rally for

> *In their darkest hours, they turned personal tragedy into public service—and in doing so they have given a legacy of love.*

Gun Elimination, a coalition of parents who work to get guns out of the hands of teenagers. Davis, who lives in Brooklyn, also formed Mothers of All Children, a support group for mothers who have experienced the painful loss.

Dee Sumpter started Mothers of Murdered Offspring, an organization that supports grieving families and increases community awareness of violence, after her 20-year-old daughter was murdered in Charlotte, North Carolina. "We as mothers are a very powerful group of people," Sumpter says. "They come from us, they lived inside of us and, because of that we have to make sure the violence, the senselessness that took them away, is not in vain."

Charlotte Austin-Jordan, Frances
Davis, Dee Sumpter and Yvonne
Pointer *(l to r)* formed organizations
to support others who are challenged
by the tragic loss of a child.

Austin-Jordan *(left)*, Sumpter *(above)* and Pointer *(opposite)* provide support to grieving families.

In Los Angeles, Charlotte Austin-Jordan's two children were murdered in a case of mistaken identity, and she lost a nephew to gang belligerence. She subsequently founded Save Our Future, an organization that counsels crime victims and works with juvenile and adult offenders. Austin-Jordan is also trying to start a dialogue between mothers and teenagers in her community about the pain that engulfs an entire family when a relative is killed. "Gangbangers have mothers, too," she says. "We've tried having fathers talk to them, police and even other gangbangers talking to them. We've never tried to get mothers to talk to them." She hopes that these personal testimonies and conversations will make a difference.

After Yvonne Pointer's 14-year-old daughter, Gloria, was raped and murdered in Cleveland, she started the support groups Parents Against Child Killings and Positive Plus, which are dedicated to the "holistic reconstruction of lives." More than 20 years after the death of her daughter, Pointer is getting on with her life: She wrote the book *Behind the Death of a Child* and lectures nationwide. "I don't make apologies for feeling happy," Pointer says. "It's a greater testimony to Gloria Pointer's life that her mother survived the grief. It didn't break me; it made me stronger."

The strength of all these women is amazing and awe-inspiring. In their darkest hours, Sumpter, Pointer, Davis and Austin-Jordan turned personal tragedy into public service—and in doing so they have given a legacy of love. ■

Sherry Grace

OUTWARDLY, Sherry Grace seemed to have it all. She and her husband, Willie, a dentist, were raising four children in a Florida suburb. She owned an interior-design business and was a leader in her church community. But the peaceful domesticity of the Grace household hid some tragic truths. Two of her three sons were caught up in a cycle of drug abuse and robbery. Eventually, the two were imprisoned—several times.

At first, Grace tried to "fix" her sons and manage their problems, but when that didn't work, she fell into despair. Finally Grace realized that the problem was bigger than she was, and opted to let go of the situation and give it up to God. After years of wearing the mask of suburban normalcy, she broke down and told her church community about her family's problems. She asked for their support in prayer, and amazing things began to happen.

As her oldest son began turning his life around, Grace realized that she wasn't alone in her pain: Hundreds, perhaps thousands, of other mothers were walking down the same painful path she had traveled—and they were walking it alone. She saw the need for understanding and healing, a place to release their anguish. So in 2001 Grace founded Mothers of Incarcerated Sons (MIS), a nonprofit, faith-based support group in Central Florida. Its more than 200 members offer support to the women who are supporting incarcerated sons, and they embrace and empower the men in prison through newsletters and regular correspondence. Working in conjunction with the area's law-enforcement agencies, MIS also helps recently released prisoners find housing and jobs and acts as an advocate for the incarcerated, regardless of their offense. Of her mission Grace says, "I have no fear because God tells me what to do. And love is more powerful than anything."

It takes courage to turn pain into something others can benefit from. Sherry Grace created a space where grief-stricken mothers and incarcerated sons could cry, argue, love each other and, ultimately, recover and heal. ■

Sherry Grace
saw the need
for a place
where mothers
of incarcerated
sons can heal
their pain.

"*I have no fear because God tells me what to do. And love is more powerful than anything.*"

3 Doctors From Newark

RAMECK HUNT, M.D. ■ GEORGE JENKINS, D.M.D. ■ SAMPSON DAVIS, M.D.

SAMPSON Davis, George Jenkins and Rameck Hunt grew up in Newark, New Jersey, at the height of the 1980s crack epidemic. Friends since grade school, the three were raised by hardworking single mothers, but they were exposed to the brutal streets. Davis served time in juvenile jail for armed robbery, Hunt for attempted murder. "To me, the experience was barbaric," Hunt says. "Never again, I told myself. I didn't want to spend my life this way."

> "Sometimes you have to step out there and believe in something you can't quite see."

"We had long conversations about our families and the crazy things we'd witnessed in our neighborhoods," says Jenkins in *The Pact*, a book they wrote about their experiences. "We also talked about school and what we wanted to do with our lives. It was clear that, like me, Sam and Rameck wanted to make something of their lives." During that time a recruiter visited Jenkins's science class and talked about the possibility of attending college free if students went into the medical field. Jenkins, who dreamed of becoming a dentist, was doubtful but interested. "Sometimes you just have to step out there and believe in something you can't quite see," he says. "And something deep down was telling me this was one of those times." Now it was a matter of getting his buddies to share the same vision. After some prodding and pushing, Davis and Hunt gave in. The trio made a pact to apply to Seton Hall University, go to college together, then go to medical school.

All three got scholarships to Seton Hall. They studied together in the evenings,

and each competed to do as well as the others. They also vowed not to lose their identity as they gained an education. "Rameck, George and I wanted to be able to enjoy college without looking or sounding like boys who went to prep school all their lives," Davis says. "We liked our 'hood' gear: baggy jeans, boots and rap music. Still do." Despite trials and temptations along the way, Davis, Jenkins and Hunt made it through.

Thirteen years after making a high-school pact to stick together and complete their education, they graduated from medical school—together. While other friends were dead or in jail or addicted to drugs, these three friends had beaten the odds. Today Dr. Davis, an emergency-room physician, Dr. Jenkins, a dentist, and Dr. Hunt, an internist, are as tight as they've ever been. They live and practice in their old community, Newark, New Jersey. ▪

Josephine Dukes

AT 103 years old Josephine Dukes is close to four decades past 65. But she just retired two years ago. Five days a week for four hours a day, the passionate centenarian was on the job in Oakland, phoning her roster of 35 senior citizens to check in on them. With a personal touch, she made sure that their heat was toasty, their refrigerators were chilling and their lives were A-OK.

When she was in her 90s, Dukes sought out the position with ASSETS, a national senior-citizen employment program, she says, to keep busy, and to keep the cash flowing. Several years before, she had lent a cousin her life savings to pay off a debt, and that was the last she saw of the money. But Dukes says she's not bitter, but rather happy to be alive and serving others. Every day her conversations are lively and full of laughter as she swaps tips on easing the aches and pains of the golden years.

> *Five days a week for four hours a day, the passionate centenarian was on the job, phoning her roster of 35 senior citizens to check in on them.*

Dukes was born in Holly Springs, Mississippi in 1902. She became a schoolteacher and later married a school principal. Dukes and her husband, Charles, moved to California in 1944 when "things began to change in the South, farmers had to cut back on their cotton production and the railroads had tickets at a reduced price." He took a job at the Alameda Naval Air Station, while she managed the rental properties they purchased. When she was widowed in the 1990s, Dukes sold her home and the properties and headed to the South again to live with a relative.

Josephine Dukes is happy to be alive.

But a year later she was back in Oakland and on her own.

Dukes is enthusiastic about living and what she still can contribute to the lives of others. "Older workers bring many positive qualities to the workplace, such as dependability, reliability and a good work ethic." she says.

Since leaving the Nation of Islam over eight years ago, Tillard has returned to his Christan roots.

Conrad Tillard

ERUDITE and outspoken, Conrad Tillard, formerly known as Conrad Muhammad, is on a mission to save young souls. The former Nation of Islam minister is trying to move young sisters and brothers to higher moral ground. His "Campaign for Decency," which focuses on the hip-hop community, calls for rap artists to alter their negative portrayals.

"I am tired of the degrading images rap is presenting about the Black race," says Tillard, who was born in Washington, D.C. "When you open up a song by calling people 'niggas' and 'niggettes,' that is not a music issue, that is a race issue. We have to fight that as vigorously as we fight the Ku Klux Klan."

One way Tillard seeks to fight it is through his youth organization, CHHANGE (Conscious Hip-Hop Activism Necessary for Global Empowerment). "If rappers boast that they are thugs and criminals and sling dope, carry pistols and spray nines, well, these activities are illegal. This Black self-criminalization gives the police justification to harass, arrest and kill our young people."

He was inspired by the role of young activists who joined with the Nation of Islam and Black Panthers in the 1960s, in their efforts to empower African-Americans.

The University of Pennsylvania graduate was inspired by the role of young activists who joined with the Nation of Islam and Black Panthers in the 1960s, in their efforts to empower African-Americans. In 1984 Muhammad's interests led him to the Nation of Islam, where he served as national youth and student spokesperson. He quickly rose through the ranks, and in 1991 he was appointed minister of Mosque #7 in Harlem.

In 2002 Tillard returned to his Christian roots, and he continues to make a greater difference in the lives of his people. ■

5

DAZZLING DYNAMOS

They have captured national attention and the admiration of millions with their own blend of can't-touch-this talent and style.

Mary J. Blige

Will & Jada Pinkett Smith

WILL Smith started his career as half of the Grammy Award–winning rap duo DJ Jazzy Jeff and the Fresh Prince. Jada Pinkett, whom he married in 1997, got her big break when she became a regular on the popular NBC sitcom *A Different World*. Today this versatile power couple has become bona fide Hollywood royalty, racking up a string of successes in film, television and music.

Growing up in Philadelphia, Will achieved early fame as a rapper. And he turned down a scholarship to study at MIT to pursue his stage ambitions, a decision that has clearly paid off. His TV hit, *The Fresh Prince of Bel-Air,* ran for six years, establishing Smith as a gifted actor with a superb sense of timing and comedic talent. From the small screen he graduated to the big one, first with *Six Degrees of Separation*. That role led to a run of megahits, including *Independence Day, Men in Black, Bad Boys* and *Hitch*. Smith won an Oscar nomination for his starring role in *Ali*.

> *This versatile power couple has become bona fide Hollywood royalty, racking up a string of successes in film, television and music.*

Jada Pinkett Smith has demonstrated her talents in more than a dozen movie roles, among them *Jason's Lyric, Set It Off* and two *Matrix* films. In addition to her acting, she's also the lead singer for Wicked Wisdom, the R&B–rock group.

Ironically, the Baltimore native once auditioned for a role in TV's *Fresh Prince* but was turned down because the producers felt that the diminutive five-foot-tall actress was too short to complement Will. Clearly, that didn't discourage future collaborations. In 2003 the pair teamed up to produce the hit UPN series *All of Us,* a family sitcom loosely based on their real-life domestic adventures.

Will and Jada Pinkett Smith are one of Hollywood's favorite couples.

Partners in love and business, they also work in tandem for humanitarian causes. Through their Will and Jada Smith Family Foundation they've donated vital financial support to community-development projects and efforts aiding underprivileged youth in their hometowns and elsewhere in the nation. And they have extended their charitable work to programs on behalf of the needy in Africa. As individual talents, Will and Jada certainly can stand on their own. But as a couple this dynamic pair is born to reign. ▪

Venus & Serena Williams

COMPTON, California, isn't exactly the tennis capital of the world, but that didn't stop Richard and Oracene Williams from teaching the sport to their youngest daughters, Venus and Serena, and telling them that one day they would be the top tennis players in the world. The lessons took. Serena played in her first tournament when she was 4; by the time Venus was 10, she had gone un-beaten in 63 games.

Venus and Serena are not just playing the game like champions; the sisters are rewriting sports history.

Today, with powerful serves that amaze audiences and daze competitors, Venus and Serena have indeed become top players in the world, with a total of more than 20 Grand Slam titles, including winning the French Open, Wimbledon, the U.S. Open and the Australian Open championships, individually and as doubles partners. Both Venus and Serena have been ranked number one in singles. They are also economic forces with multimillion-dollar endorsement deals. Off the courts, they keep busy with their own design businesses.

But the world didn't always see things the Williamses' way. Conventional wisdom had it that in order to succeed on the pro circuit, preteens and teens should first play the junior circuit. Their father thought differently. In 1996 he took Venus off the junior circuit so she could concentrate on her studies. The tennis

The Williams sisters dominate their opponents with power and finesse. Their parents, Oracene and Richard, instilled in their daughters a belief in themselves, coupled with a hard work ethic, which helped catapult them to the top of the tennis world. Talent, style and grace have made Venus and Serena fan favorites.

establishment lambasted him, saying that he was limiting her potential. Richard reasoned that Venus already had ample competition: Serena.

Venus and Serena are not just playing the game like champions; the sisters are rewriting sports history. ◼

Samuel L. Jackson

SAMUEL L. Jackson may be considered the epitome of cool, but it's the actor's passion and intensity that has made him one of Hollywood's most sought-after award-winning performers. With more than 75 roles to his credit, he is in the pantheon of character actors who bring complexity, compassion and courage to their roles.

> *Samuel L. Jackson's personal strength keeps him clear, focused and a shining star.*

Once upon a time Jackson found himself in less than winning situations. Drug addiction nearly dimmed his star in 1985. "I was tired; I just wanted to lie down and give up," he has said. "They talk about reaching your bottom, and I guess that's what happened to me." Jackson has shown great courage by publicly acknowledging the addiction that almost destroyed him—and the love and support from family that saved him.

With a new fresh outlook Jackson started on the road to superstardom. The roles have been coming ever since. From a Bible-quoting hit man (*Pulp Fiction*) to an avenging father (*A Time to Kill*), a philandering husband (*Eve's Bayou*) and Black private eye (*Shaft*), he takes on every part with an honesty and integrity that give singular voice to the Black-male experience.

Winner of the Cannes Film Festival Best Supporting Actor Award and the New York Film Critics Circle Supporting Actor Award for *Jungle Fever*, as well as an Academy Award nominee for *Pulp Fiction*, Jackson is one of the hardest working actors in the business. He has broken Hollywood's color barrier, often playing roles originally not written for Black actors, most famously as a Jedi master in three of the blockbuster *Star Wars* movies.

Husband to actress LaTanya Richardson and father to their daughter, Zoe, Samuel L. Jackson uses his personal strength to keep him clear, focused and a shining star. ▪

Mary J. Blige

MARY Jane Blige grew up in a Yonkers, New York, housing project nicknamed Slow Bomb. There was always drama on tap, the perfect environment for a girl to take up with bad company. By eleventh grade, those bad influences caught up with Blige. That was when she dropped out of high school. She wrestled with alcohol, drugs and dangerous men during those turbulent years. "When I turned 16, I just wanted to do dumb stuff and hang out," she said. "Then 20 years old rolled around and I was still doing stupid stuff."

> "Once you have self-knowledge and figure out love is the key to drawing good things to you, you glow."

But Blige, who was a choirgirl, never lost the little light inside and was determined to let it shine one day. She knew she had a voice that could move one of the toughest audiences—the members of her church—and she figured that maybe others might want to hear it too.

In a karaoke booth at a local mall, Blige recorded a version of Anita Baker's "Caught Up in the Rapture" and gave it to her stepfather, who knew somebody who knew somebody. When the tape finally landed in the office of Andre Harrell, who was the president of the Uptown Records, suddenly it was all about Mary.

Since her wildly successful first album, *What's the 411?*, which sold 2 million copies within weeks of its release, Blige has been a consistent force in

Mary J. Blige strikes an emotional cord with her fans.

the music industry. A pioneer, she took the soulful R&B of her mother's era and added beats from her own generation to help create the phenomenon known as hip-hop soul. Some say she's the queen.

"I just don't believe I went through hell for nothing," Blige has said. "I have a lot of inner power now. Once you have self-knowledge and figure out that love is the key to drawing good things to you, you glow." ▪

Tyra Banks

SINCE the early 1990's, her stunning looks have made her a runway and fashion media star, helping her snag lucrative contracts representing companies like Victoria's Secret and Cover Girl. But Tyra Banks—also a savvy enterprising woman—says she's always known that her fate could never hinge simply on looking good and walking the runway.

"I want to be in charge of myself, in control of my career," says Banks. "You can be a businesswoman and a producer long after the boobs have fallen and the looks have faded. And that's what real power is all about."

With her mother, Carolyn London, at the helm of her company, she's branching out in ways that allow her to build a strong financial base. Her hit reality show, *America's Next Top Model,* which Banks created, produces and hosts, entered its fifth installment in 2005, when she also launched *The Tyra Banks Show,* a daytime TV talk show.

> *Banks is a great businesswoman, mentor and role model.*

In many ways Banks has come full circle. Before becoming a runway goddess, Tyra was an insecure child tormented by a condition causing her skin to erupt. Later she underwent a growth spurt that led to her being teased so much she would hide in her bedroom. At the urging of friends and family Banks began to pursue modeling. She was about to enter college when she landed a modeling job in Paris. She took the job to pay for school, but modeling blossomed into a career.

In 1999 she formed the Tzone Foundation, which sponsors a camp where girls can learn to value themselves more. Not content to be a model only, Banks has turned herself into a phenomenal businesswoman, mentor and role model. And she's doing it in ways that she can bank on. ■

James Blake

THERE'S so much to honor and admire in the life of our tennis-playing brother James Blake. A year before he made his way to the 2005 United States Open, a physically and emotionally battered Blake often wondered what would become of his professional tennis career. During one brutal three-month period in 2004, his entire world seemed to fall apart. In May of that year, Blake crashed into a net post, and he broke his neck. In July he lost his father, Thomas, to stomach cancer. Shortly afterward, James was diagnosed with the stress-related virus Zoster. It impaired his vision and caused a temporary paralysis of his face. "I kept thinking, *I wonder if I'll ever be able to play again.*"

He proved to himself and to his fans that in the game of life he is a winner.

Not only would Blake play again, but his great comeback is of legend. Blessed with a strong can-do attitude, 26-year-old Blake won one of the last tournaments before the U.S. Open. But at the 2005 U.S. Open he showed the world the tough stuff he was made of. The unseeded underdog tore through the 164-man field, becoming one of the last eight players standing.

Born in Yonkers, New York, and raised in Connecticut, Blake seemed destined to play tennis no matter what. His father would take him and his older brother, Thomas Jr., to the Harlem Junior Tennis Program. When James was 13 he was stricken with scoliosis, and for a while, he spent 18 hours a day wearing a back brace. It put a halt to his game. Blake returned to playing and became an All American at Harvard and the nation's top-ranked collegiate player.

Blake credits his father with inspiring him to keep up his drive. "That's why when I'm done playing tennis, I'm still going to find other things to challenge myself." Whatever he does, we can count on him doing it with determination and style. ■

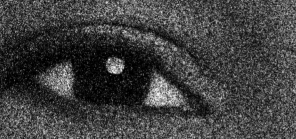

6

SPIRIT LIFTERS

Their lives and messages embody inspiration—and demonstrate the power of love.

Iyanla Vanzant

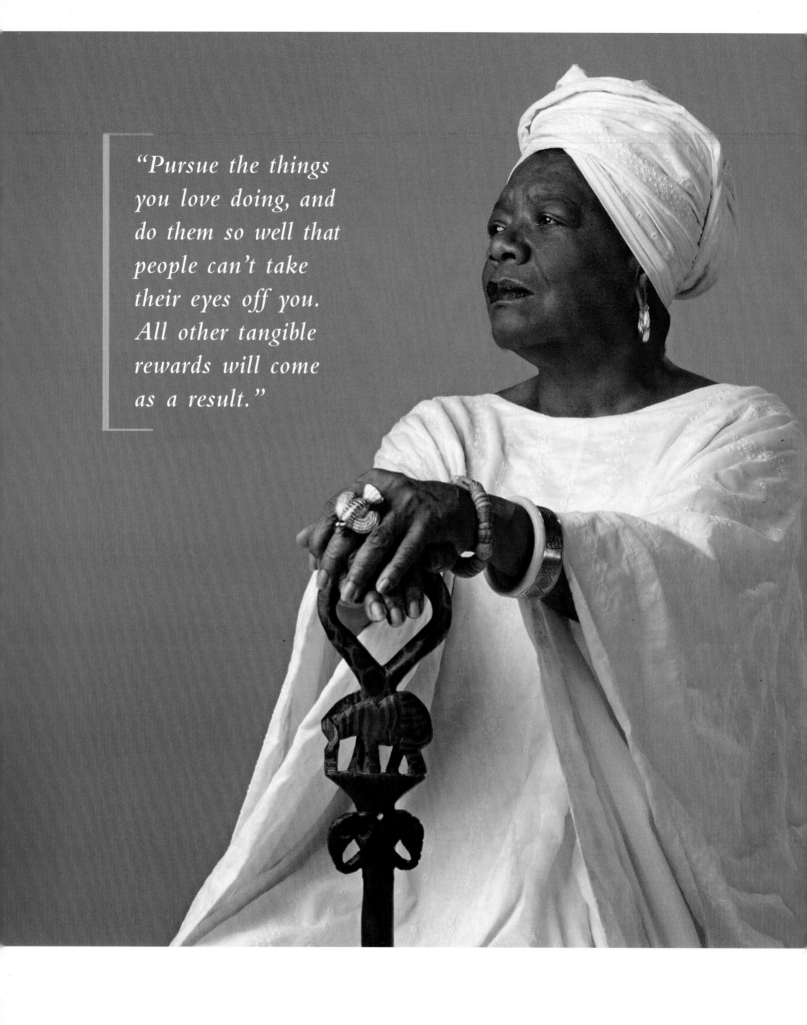

"Pursue the things you love doing, and do them so well that people can't take their eyes off you. All other tangible rewards will come as a result."

Maya Angelou

TO Black America she is Queen Mother, treasured for her eloquence and elegance and her bold self-acceptance and openhearted love of others. She looks exactly how we imagine many an African queen would: tall, stately, head high, carriage erect, eyes wide, a quiet sense of confidence exuding from her body. Maya Angelou is our beloved writer, actress, poet, director of works for the stage and screen, singer, dancer and professor.

As a writer, Angelou has stirred the hearts of millions of readers with her first book, *I Know Why the Caged Bird Sings*, which chronicled the pain of her childhood years. But in subsequent memoirs covering her adult years and in her poetry and essays, Angelou always seeks to shed light on the human experience. She made her feature directorial debut in 1998 with *Down in the Delta*, starring Wesley Snipes and Alfre Woodard. In short, she has an abundance of gifts, of which she takes great joy in sharing. Of her life achievements, Angelou, who was born in St. Louis and makes her home in Winston-Salem, North Carolina, says, "Don't make money your goal. Instead pursue the things you love doing, and do them so well that people can't take their eyes off you. All other tangible rewards will come as a result."

In the 1960s she served as northern coordinator for the Southern Christian Leadership Conference at the request of Dr. Martin Luther King. And over the last few decades, she has been appointed to key committees by Presidents Ford and Carter. In 1993, at the request of President Clinton, she became only the second poet ever—Robert Frost was the first—to write and recite an original work at a presidential inauguration. Wake Forest University in Winston-Salem clearly demonstrated that they knew she was a keeper: In 1981 they appointed Dr. Angelou to a lifetime position as their first Reynolds Professor of American Studies.

With Maya Angelou, we are always learning. She teaches by example: how to be more graceful, gracious and giving; the importance of giving praise, honor and respect; and living wholly, fully in the world. ■

> Maya Angelou has an abundance of gifts, and she takes great joy in sharing them.

Treasured for her eloquence and elegance, Maya Angelou's writings shed light on the human experience.

Despite the hurdles, Asgedom had faith that the future could be as bright as the past had been dim.

Mawi Asgedom

MAWI Asgedom's resilient spirit has taken him from a refugee camp in Sudan to earning a bachelor's degree from Harvard University, and he's still stepping. He was only 3 years old when his family fled from their home on the border of Eritrea and Ethiopia to escape a deadly civil war. But today, Asgedom shares his life story to inspire others. He has become a powerful motivational speaker and is much in demand around the country and has authored three books.

Living in a refugee camp, his family faced hunger and disease. They couldn't go home, but they couldn't live a good life in the camp either. So their next move was to the United States when Mawi was 7. The Asgedoms lived in hotels around Chicago, until they established a place of their own. Here, there was a confusing new language and customs to learn, as well as confronting the overall culture shock of living in a strange land. It was a time of enormous sacrifice: Mawi's father, who had been a doctor back home, became a janitor.

Despite the hurdles, Asgedom had faith that the future could be as bright as the past had been dim. He studied hard and excelled in school. When it was time to apply to colleges, Asgedom applied to Harvard. Not only did Harvard accept him, but also the school offered him a full scholarship. In 1999, when he graduated cum laude, he was selected as one of the four graduation speakers. And on graduation day, he addressed a crowd of 30,000. It was a bittersweet moment. Mawi Asgedom's father and brother were not there to celebrate with him; both had been killed by drunk drivers, six years apart.

Some of the proceeds from his book, *Of Beetles and Angels: A Boy's Remarkable Journey From a Refugee Camp to Harvard*, go to the HAT Foundation, named for his father and brother, Haileab and Tewolde. Mawi keeps them, along with the people of his African homeland, in his heart as his journey continues. ■

> Moving to a strange land with his parents, brother and two sisters, Mawi Asgedom had to learn a new language and customs.

Through her institute,
Inner Visions Spiritual
Life and Maintenance
Center, Iyanla Vanzant
empowers individuals
to better their lives.

Iyanla Vanzant

> "I am just
> an ordinary person
> committed to doing
> extraordinary things."

WHERE there is inspiration, there is Iyanla. She is our proof that recovery from victimization and self-doubt is not only possible but is also ours to have if we tap into our personal power and "inner Black wealth." Born in a taxi in Brooklyn, this nationally known spiritual teacher and minister went from an abusive marriage, postpartum depression and confinement in a psychiatric ward to transforming herself into one of the nation's most powerful public speakers. The author of 11 best-selling books—five of which made *The New York Times* best-seller list—she founded the Inner Visions Spiritual Life and Maintenance Center in Silver Springs, Maryland. But at the root of Vanzant's multimillion-dollar enterprise is a divinely simple mission: to help women lift themselves from challenging circumstances.

Vanzant's soul opened up in 1974 in the psychiatric ward of a Brooklyn hospital, where she was recovering from a suicide attempt four weeks after giving birth to her daughter Nisa. After her release (and with less than $5 in her pocket), the woman who was born Rhonda Harris in 1953 began studying many faiths and cultures, including the Yoruba people of West Africa. She took the name Iyanla ("great mother") after becoming a Yoruba high priestess in 1983. A few years later she put herself through law school, and by the time she was 35, Vanzant was working as a public defender in Philadelphia. While there she realized her true calling and seized it with a passion that only keeps growing.

In 1988 Vanzant founded Inner Visions, a national personal-growth institute, where she trains holistic practitioners to fulfill the mission of empowering all individuals. Several years later she penned her first book, *Acts of Faith: Daily Meditations for People of Color*. Hungry for her brand of mother wit and spiritual truths, African-Americans and many people of other races embraced Iyanla's teachings, propelling

her meteoric climb to the top of her own empire. Ten more books followed, and so did regular guest appearances on *The Oprah Winfrey Show* from 1998 to 1999, which brought her to national acclaim and television fame.

At 46 Vanzant pursued a master's degree in spiritual psychology. Now "ministering" her brand of sister-girl healing to women globally, including prisoners, Iyanla Vanzant is a woman whose passion for personal development has transformed so many. "I know who I am," she says, "and I'm clear about my purpose. I am just an ordinary person committed to doing extraordinary things." ■

Iyanla Vanzant's mission is to help women lift themselves from challenging circumstances.

Michael Eric Dyson

A bridge between God and gangsta rap, Michael Eric Dyson—scholar, minister, author and lecturer—is also one of the most brilliant cultural critics of his generation. From pulpits to campuses, he examines the Black experience—breaking down the dynamics of religious rapture, racism and rap music with equal dexterity.

> *From pulpits to campuses, he examines the Black experience—breaking down the dynamics of religious rapture, racism and rap music with equal dexterity.*

Dyson began acquiring his street savvy at the age of 9, when he and his older brother joined the Stanford Street gang in Detroit and became enmeshed in violence and the street ethics of respect, revenge and retaliation. After graduating from high school, he became a teenage father and underwent a personal resurrection. His pastor, Dr. Frederick Sampson at the Tabernacle Mission Baptist Church, became the mentor Dyson so desperately needed, providing him with enough spiritual ammunition to alter his convictions and sharply turn his life around. "He gave me a powerful and vivid image of what a responsible Black leader and minister should be to his people that has stayed with me to this day," says Dyson, who went on to receive master's and doctoral degrees in religion from Princeton University. He became a Baptist minister and a professor of religious studies at the University of North Carolina at Chapel Hill, and eventually the director of the Institute of African-American Research. Along the way, he also began mixing liturgy with a critical analysis of hip-hop and the genre's lyrics into his lectures.

Dyson has explored racism, sexism and popular culture in several best-selling books, including *Race Rules: Navigating the Color Line*. Committed to higher learn-

ing, he became the Ida B. Wells-Barnett Professor of Religious Studies at DePaul University, then in 2002 was appointed the Avalon Foundation Professor in Humanities at the University of Pennsylvania. Much of Dyson's research has focused on the Black church and the contemporary crises facing African-Americans. For many African-Americans his greatest gift is the continuation of the important legacy of Black preachers—tending to spiritual matters, denouncing social and political injustices, and speaking to the powerful as well as the power-less. Michael Eric Dyson and his wife, the Reverend Marcia Dyson, continue to uplift our community—one person in need at a time. ■

Michael Eric Dyson focuses on the Black church and on contemporary crises facing the African-American community.

Yolanda Adams

YOLANDA Adams is intent on making a joyful noise unto the Lord. And she's intent on taking her musical ministry—the marriage of traditional gospel music with elements of R&B—to as many people as possible. With best-selling albums and an armful of awards to her credit, it is clear that Adams is being heard.

Even as a girl, Adams wasn't shy about sharing her talent. She began singing in her church when she was 7, and in the rocky teen years following her father's untimely death, singing with a regional choir helped soothe her sadness. Through the ups and downs of her life, she kept raising her voice in song. She was settled into a career as a teacher for seven years when one day, while singing a solo with the choir, Adams was discovered by the owner of a small gospel record company. A dozen years later, Elektra signed her on as its first nonsecular artist.

"I'm not out to change gospel music. I just want to give God his just due, and my goal is to show people how really cool God is."

Her debut record for Elektra, *Mountain High, Valley Low*, which featured the hit single "Open My Heart," went platinum, and a string of tributes followed. Adams has stayed true to her gospel roots, incorporating into her music a blend of the styles she listened to as a child: the nuanced phrasing of a Nancy Wilson is juxtaposed with the funk and spontaneity of a Stevie Wonder and the ethereal quality of a Donny Hathaway. Somehow, it works.

Adams brings elegance and high style to her performances, but she says that doesn't make her message any less valid. "I'm not out to change gospel music," says the songtress. "I just want to give God his just due, and my goal is to show people how really cool God is." By doing what she loves, and staying true to her gospel roots, Yolanda Adams is accomplishing her mission. ■

Adams exudes grace and spirit in her musical message.

Yolanda
Adams
incorporates
into her
gospel music
a blend of
styles she
listened to
as a child.

Bishop T.D. Jakes

BISHOP T.D. Jakes is healing the souls of Black folks. Not only does he head a Dallas-based megachurch with 30,000 members, but he has also become one of the nation's most influential Christian leaders. Millions turn to his books for inspiration. And his TV ministry reaches across color lines to help people heal the past, make peace with the present and create a powerful future.

His faith first took root in the rich soil of South Charleston, West Virginia, where he was brought up by his mother, a home-economics teacher, and his father, who owned a successful janitorial business. Young Jakes would give sermons to imaginary congregations in his family's backyard, and he carted his Bible every-

Black people are filling up to 52,000 seats to hear T.D. Jakes's resounding sermons at conferences around the country.

where. He started his first church when he was 22 years old. With spirit to spare, he also took to the airwaves, hosting a radio show called *The Master's Plan.*

Jakes's messages have always centered on healing and renewal, in part because he watched his father struggle with kidney disease. He was 16 when his father died. "My ability to understand people who are hurting has to do with visiting a hospital so often when I was growing up and talking with kids who were dying around me," the bishop says.

During college and after, Jakes divided his time between preaching and serving as music director at the Baptist church in which he was raised. It wasn't until 1982 that he put all his energy into his ministry.

His reputation flourished, and so did his flock. By 1996 he and his wife, Serita, and their five children, along with 50 other families, had relocated to Dallas, founding the Potter's House, a ministry which sits on 28 acres of rolling hills in Dallas's Oak Cliff area. Black people are embracing his message in ever-increasing numbers and filling up to 52,000 seats to hear his resounding sermons at conferences around the country. His first and most popular book, *Woman Thou Art Loosed!*, is one of his five best sellers and was adapted into a feature film that speaks directly to the hearts of hurting women.

"I try to provide some biblical answers to sociological ills," Jakes says. "If we don't learn to manage pain by dissolving it or letting it go, it infects the future." And Bishop Jakes isn't about to let that happen. ■

7

HEALERS & TEACHERS

Through education and medicine, they are nurturing minds and saving lives.

Keith Black

Ben Carson, M.D.

THE world-renowned neurosurgeon Dr. Benjamin Carson has taken on cases that no other doctor would touch. He has saved many a child's life by operating on their brains to stop seizures and to remove cancer. In 1986 he became the first neurosurgeon to perform surgery on a twin baby while both infants were still in the womb. But it was the 1987 surgery in which he separated conjoined twins in Germany that catapulted the doctor to celebrity status.

When Carson, now the director of Pediatric Neurosurgery at Johns Hopkins Medical Center, was a child, he suffered from low self-esteem. Growing up poor in 1950s Detroit, money was in short supply, especially after his parents, Robert and Sonya Carson, split up when Ben was 8 years old. At school, Ben and his brother, Curtis, struggled to keep their attention on their schoolwork, but their grades sank. That only served to stir up cruel racial slurs about how their color contributed to their low marks.

But their mother, who was working as a domestic in three jobs, was determined to bring the best out of her boys. Sonya Carson limited the time her sons spent watching television, sent them to the library often and demanded that they read two books a week. Their grades improved, but the brothers still faced a hostile environment. One teacher chastised the White students for allowing Ben to win an achievement award. That indignity, he says, and others filled him with rage. "I would fly off the handle," he once recalled. One day he tried to stab a boy in the stomach, but fortunately, the blade hit the youngster's belt buckle. Carson knew he had to change his behavior, so he turned

> *"I started reading the Book of Proverbs, and three hours later, I had a different view of the world."*

Ben Carson is the author of three celebrated books, including *Gifted Hands.*

to the Bible. "I started reading the Book of Proverbs," he says. "When I came out three hours later, I had a different view of the world."

Carson rededicated himself to his studies and did so well in high school that he won a scholarship to Yale University. After graduating with a degree in psychology he went on to the University of Michigan School of Medicine. Carson realized that he had a gift for surgery. He has been celebrated for his precision and compassion. His touch applied to desperately ill babies around the globe saves them, while bringing relief to their parents.

Carson with his wife, Candy, created the Carson Scholars Fund to help grade school and high school academic stars go to college. He is intent on motivating others the way his mother had motivated him. ▪

Ruth Simmons

IT'S a safe bet that Ruth Simmons, president of Brown University, is the first, last and only Ivy League university president born in a sharecropper's shack. The youngest of 12 siblings with roots in the dusty, rural poverty of Grapeland, Texas, Simmons was 15 when her mother died. If anyone could use humble beginnings as an excuse for not making it in the world, she could.

In her youth, however, Simmons discovered something she was passionate about, something that led her out of her childhood circumstances into a brighter future: education. Today Simmons can claim a number of firsts: the first African-American to be named president of Smith College, the elite women's school, and the first African-American to become president of an Ivy League institution, Brown University.

That these top schools chose Simmons is a tribute to her tenacity and her thirst for knowledge. But it's also a testament to the people of Grapeland, especially the teachers who recognized her potential and refused to let her fall through the cracks. These educators encouraged her to read and join community organizations and after-school clubs, and when she won a scholarship to Dillard University, they took up a collection so that she'd have a coat to wear when she got there.

After graduating summa cum laude from Dillard, Simmons went on to Harvard, where she received a master's degree and a doctorate in romance languages. She held academic posts at Spelman College and Princeton University

> *"I'd like for every student to experience a moment of learning that is so delicious that they want to hold on to it forever."*

As the first African-American president of an Ivy League university, Simmons believes in the value of education.

before being named president of Smith in 1995. Six years later, when Brown University called, the divorced mother of two children answered.

It's no surprise that Ruth Simmons believes in the power of education: "I'd like for every student to experience a moment of learning that is so delicious that they want to hold on to it forever," she says. ▨

Dikembe Mutombo

DURING the basketball season NBA center Dikembe Mutombo is a star athlete. Off-season he uses his success as a professional basketball player to provide health care for the people in his African homeland, Democratic Republic of the Congo.

As a youngster Mutombo wanted to be a doctor. He attended Georgetown University on a USAID scholarship, but after graduating in 1991, his great height, speed and agility landed him in the NBA with the Denver Nuggets, followed by stints in Atlanta, Philadelphia, New Jersey, New York and Houston. His good fortune has allowed him to give the people in the Congo the medical support they so desperately need.

"When you take the elevator up to the top, please don't forget to send it back down so that someone else can take it up."

With a population of more than 40 million, the Congo has what Mutombo considers one of the worst health conditions in Africa. In 1997 he established the Dikembe Mutombo Foundation to help improve health, education and the quality of life in the country. Through Mutombo's support, the foundation has delivered hundreds of beds and millions of dollars worth of medical and pharmaceutical supplies to the Congo. Yet in 1998, his own mother died because she could not reach a hospital in time. This painful loss spurred Mutombo's commitment to do more. In 2000 he gave $3.5 million to establish a new hospital in Kinshasa, the country's capital.

Dikembe Mutombo shares his success by supporting medical needs in his homeland, the Congo, formerly Zaire.

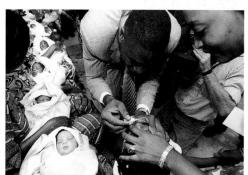

Mutombo often quotes a Central African proverb, words that he himself lives by, "When you take the elevator up to the top, please don't forget to send it back down so that someone else can take it up." ∎

Shirley Ann Jackson

IN July 1999 physicist Shirley Ann Jackson, Ph.D. was inaugurated as the eighteenth president of Rensselaer Polytechnic Institute—a historical event witnessed by thousands of people, including Senator Hillary Rodham Clinton.

> *She is the first African-American woman to lead a national research university.*

Jackson is the first African-American woman to lead a national research university.

In 1998 Jackson was inducted into the National Women's Hall of Fame for her contributions as a scientist and as an advocate for education, science and public policy. Her career is distinguished by historic firsts. In 1973 she became the first African-American woman to receive a doctorate from the Massachusetts Institute of Technology (MIT). She was one of the first two African-American women in the United States to have earned a doctorate in physics from any university and the first Black woman elected to the National Academy of Engineering. In 1995 she became the first African-American and first woman appointed as commissioner of the U.S. Nuclear Regulatory Commission.

In her several years of leadership at Rensselaer, Jackson has continued her trailblazing efforts, working to secure the institution as a world-class research university. ■

Shirley Ann Jackson was the first African-American woman to receive a Ph.D. from MIT.

Keith Black, M.D.

KEITH Black, M.D., dares to unravel the mysteries of life. As director of the Maxine Dunitz Neurosurgical Institute at Cedars-Sinai Medical Center in Los Angeles, Black leads the medical charge in the "tumor wars" against brain cancer. Armed with a scalpel, a steady hand, keen intelligence and a dizzying array of technology, Black is known for his unerring dexterity in excising malignant brain tumors. Since 1987 he has performed more than 3,000 operations, and he is one of a select group of surgeons in the United States who specialize in the medical condition. Black is revered internationally as well: Many of his patients come from Europe, South America, Japan, the Middle East and Australia.

> *Dr. Keith Black says he is "simply God's instrument."*

Ever since his medical-school days at the University of Michigan, Ann Arbor, Black has been fascinated by what he calls the sacredness of the brain. "If you want to understand the artist, you study his art," he says. "If you want to understand God, you study the anatomy of the brain."

Black, a native of Auburn, Alabama, is humble and understandably uncomfortable when grateful patients whose lives he has saved tell him he is God. No one is more aware than this esteemed surgeon that he is, as he states, "simply God's instrument." ∎

Randall Robinson

FOR decades Randall Robinson has stood on the front lines to ensure justice for people of African ancestry throughout the world. The founder of TransAfrica, an advocacy organization that has spearheaded the movement for influencing U.S. politics toward international Black leadership, Robinson speaks out on issues that affect Black people globally. He started TransAfrica in 1977 to address the absence of African voices in international policy and the general neglect of Black countries. Under his direction, the group worked tirelessly to keep Africa and the Caribbean high on the United States' foreign-policy agenda. In protesting American policy toward Haiti, Robinson staged a 27-day hunger strike to force the United States to halt its discriminatory practices against Haitian refugees. The strike landed him in a hospital, but it also resulted in a policy reversal.

"You fight prepared to go the long term, and if your life won't cover the term of the struggle, then you hand off your progress to the next generation."

Raised in Richmond, he started his political activism while at Virginia Union University and Harvard Law School. He joined campus protests against apartheid in South Africa, and later a visit to that country showed him the crushing conditions he had been fighting against. He became even more committed to reform.

Robinson has also committed his life, works and philosophies to the printed page. He is the author of *Defending the Spirit*, his memoirs. In *The Debt: What America Owes to Blacks*, he calls for reparations for descendants of enslaved Blacks. "It is not difficult to argue that when you expropriate the value of a people's labor for 246 years of slavery, and follow that with a century of formal discrimination, those who were in the beneficiary group stood to gain and those who

Randall
Robinson's
latest
book is
*Quitting
America.*

had the value of their lives stolen from them stood to suffer," says Robinson. He and other lawyers and scholars, including Cornel West and the late Johnnie Cochran, have filed lawsuits to remedy years of unpaid labor.

Robinson, who moved to the island of St. Kitts in 2001, says, "I put no clock on these things. I don't know if it will happen in my lifetime, in the same way I didn't know if apartheid would end in my lifetime, the same way I didn't know if Aristide believed he would go home to a liberated Haiti. But you fight prepared to go the long term, and if your life won't cover the term of the struggle, then you hand off your progress to the next generation." ∎

Neil deGrasse Tyson

NEIL deGrasse Tyson always aimed for the stars, even when it wasn't cool to do so in his Bronx neighborhood. Tyson, who became the youngest director in the history of the world-class Hayden Planetarium in New York City, has over the past several years become the nation's most recognized astronomer, astrophysicist and author in his field. He is admired by his peers for his ability to translate complex cosmic phenomena into something everyday people can grasp.

Tyson started attracting national attention in 1983 when he began writing a Q&A column for *Star Date*, a science magazine, shortly after graduating from the

Neil deGrasse Tyson always aimed for the stars, even when it wasn't cool to do so in his Bronx neighborhood.

University of Texas at Austin, where he had received a master's degree in physics. Six years later, while he was studying for his Ph.D. in astrophysics at Columbia University, Tyson's columns became a book, *Merlin's Tour of the Universe*. Research at Princeton University followed, inspiring the prolific writer to pen a monthly column in *Natural History* magazine and seven more books, including an autobiography, *The Sky Is Not the Limit*. In the autobiography, readers learned of Tyson's many accomplishments and that even with his credentials he has endured countless indignities from "suspicious cops, shop owners, cabbies and cocktail-party bores" because of his skin color. As an African-American scientist, Tyson also acknowledges that more is expected of him simply because of his race. "There's an extra social tax I have to pay," he explains. "It's not a burden. I just pay the tax."

Neil deGrasse Tyson, who began studying the moon through a pair of binoculars at age 9, always makes himself available to children visiting the planetarium, exposing future generations to the wonders of science. ▪

Neil deGrasse Tyson works to promote science education for underserved children in New York City.

8

NEXT GENERATION

Young achievers are making it happen and already have left their unique marks in our communities.

Raven-Symoné

AT the tender age of 20, multitalented Raven has done so much. We've watched her blossom from precocious little Olivia on *The Cosby Show* to her current starring role in the hugely successful Disney channel series *That's So Raven*. She's acted alongside Eddie Murphy in both hit *Dr. Dolittle* movies, had a four-year run in the popular sitcom *Hanging With Mr. Cooper* and starred in the TV film *The Cheetah Girls*. A versatile young star, Raven-Symoné has released two CDs, and she's inspired a *That's So Raven*–themed video game. Yet, for all the time she's spent on center stage, she's remained refreshingly grounded.

> *If Raven seems to wear her stardom with ease, perhaps it's because she's only doing what comes naturally.*

Popular media offers young girls of color precious few positive and healthy role models. That alone is reason to celebrate Raven's unprecedented success. She's funny and cool and has plenty of style. And if Raven seems to wear her stardom with ease, perhaps it's because she's only doing what comes naturally. Born in Atlanta but raised in New York, by the time she was 3 she'd already had a modeling contract and an assignment to audition for the Bill Cosby movie *Ghost Dad*. She was too young for the part, so Cosby snapped her up to play one of his Cosby kids.

In her current series, which is a Disney channel daily staple, Raven gets to flaunt her talent as a zany comedienne. Her character's ability to see into the future always lands her in some kind of jam, which usually requires some wacky maneuvering to sort out. Raven's capers have attracted a flock of loyal young fans who've made the show top-rated among the nation's girls between the ages of 9 and 14.

It's all helping to transform Raven into a highly lucrative brand. She has fragrance and clothing lines in the works, and in 2006 Disney is looking to sell nearly $400 million in Raven-themed bedding, lunch boxes, lamps and dolls. Move over, Snow White and Cinderella. Let's make room for some real girl power. ■

Above: Raven has lots of fans, including those at a bookstore event she attended for Cheetah Girls. Opposite page: A Raven doll was created as one of many products inspired by the popular young entertainer.

With her mother,
Patricia Broadbent,
Hydeia is the author
of *You Can Get Past
the Tears: A Memoir
of Love and Survival.*

Hydeia L. Broadbent

AT first glance, Hydeia L. Broadbent looks like a typical 21 year old. But she was born HIV-positive and has had AIDS since she was 5. In fact, she is one of thousands of young people in the United States with AIDS. Yet activism can grow from tragedy, and Hydeia has become an eloquent spokesperson through the Hydeia L. Broadbent Foundation, started by her mother in 1995 in Los

> *She brings a message of hope, encouragement and love to those affected by AIDS.*

Angeles. She lectures regularly at schools and universities around the country, has appeared on television talk shows and spoke at the Republican National Convention in 1996. She brings a message of hope, encouragement and love to those affected by the disease.

Hydeia was born to a drug-using mother who abandoned her at birth. She was adopted at 5 weeks by Patricia and Loren Broadbent, whose steadfast love and you-can-do-anything support gave Hydeia the wings to soar. They gave her the love and care all children deserve. Now not only living with AIDS but also thriving, the courageous young woman has shown how a determined family can defy even the grimmest odds.

Several years ago at Hydeia's urging, the Las Vegas couple, who have six other children, took in two other kids with AIDS. Hydeia's example ultimately shows that a child can lead us. ∎

Kenya Jordana James

SIXTEEN-year-old Kenya Jordana James was 10 when she noticed that there were no magazines that addressed her interests and concerns, so she took action. As an African-American preteen, she didn't see much of herself in teen magazines, and the adult ones featured articles her mother wouldn't let her read. With her mother's help, James did some research, put together an editorial plan and created a test issue of a magazine for young Black girls, using $1,200 she had earned from selling home-baked goods. Dozens of telephone calls, pitch letters and rejections later, things started to gel. From the basement of her Atlanta home, at the ripe old age of 12, James produced a 20-page premier issue of *Blackgirl*, a bimonthly magazine for young sisters.

> *"This magazine is a way for me to give back to my community, by offering a magazine that girls— like me—have been looking for."*

Kenya James displays vision and drive. After 3,000 copies of the first issue sold out, James printed 5,000 copies of the second and third issues. And she has snagged personal interviews for *Blackgirl* with major artists including Jill Scott, Outkast, Bow Wow and Lauryn Hill. *Blackgirl* also features articles on history, culture, education and style. A group of teenage volunteers help James get the job done. "This magazine is a way for me to give back to my community, by offering a magazine that girls—like me—have been looking for," James says. "We have a lot to say."

And in *Blackgirl*, little sis has provided them with a place to say it. ■

PHOTOGRAPHY CREDITS

INDEX